Song of Love

Song of Love

A Biblical Understanding of Sex

HELMUT GOLLWITZER

Translated by Keith Crim

FORTRESS PRESS   *Philadelphia*

Library of Congress Cataloging in Publication Data

Gollwitzer, Helmut.
    Song of love.

    Translation of Das hohe Lied der Liebe.
    Includes bibliographical references.
    1. Sex (Theology)—Biblical teaching. 2. Bible.
O. T. Song of Solomon—Theology. I. Title.
BS680.S5G5813   241'.6'6   78-14667
ISBN 0-8006-1360-0

7402K78   Printed in the United States of America   1–533

. . . about the Song of Songs—I actually prefer to read it as a worldly love song.
—Dietrich Bonhoeffer

Contents

Preface		9
1.	Sexual Love—Human or Divine?	11
2.	Allegorical and Historical Interpretation	15
3.	The Affirmation of Sexual Love	25
4.	Sexual Desire—God's Good Gift	33
5.	Ordering Sexual Relationship	39
6.	Sex, Eros, and Agape	45
7.	Sex and Society	61
8.	The Song of Songs— A Magna Charta of Humanity	71
	Notes	77

Preface

At the seventeenth Kirchentag, a week-long festival held in Berlin 8–12 June 1977 under the auspices of the German Evangelical Church, thousands of Christians and non-Christians of many sorts, mostly laity, gathered to consider and discuss the meaning and implications of Christian faith for the daily life of individuals, church, and society. Besides lectures, discussions, and worship experiences, each day's agenda featured intensive periods of Bible study, the first two days on chapters 12 and 13 of Paul's First Letter to the Corinthians.

The ''Christians and Jews'' study group asked if I would present some reflections on the Song of Songs, the Old Testament book traditionally ascribed to King Solomon. They specifically wanted me to relate that book to the famous Pauline ''hymn to love'' in 1 Corinthians 13.

Over the years of the Kirchentag this study group had established the stimulating practice of inviting both a Christian and a Jew to address themselves to the common theme. My partner in Berlin on 11 June was Pinchas

Lapide, whose wisdom, learning, and enthusiasm had long been dedicated to the cause of enhanced Christian-Jewish understanding. Our dialogue was followed with great interest by a large group of listeners who then pursued in smaller discussion sections the questions we had raised in the larger assembly.

Although there were areas of considerable agreement between Lapide and myself, there is no denying the fact that lively disagreements also emerged. Lapide sees in the Song of Songs poetic praise of *married* love, whereas I follow the lead of Gillis Gerleman and other modern scholars in finding that view unsupported by the text itself. Our differences on this score opened up the whole question of whether sexual love depends for its legitimacy on some kind of authorization by society and church. The question remains acute, and not just for Dr. Lapide and myself or those attending the Kirchentag.

In preparing for those Berlin discussions I wrote out the results of my study and reflection on the Song of Songs. Although the actual writing was a bit hurried, done while I was journeying through France, it is offered here nonetheless. During that trip I found myself changing some opinions and formulations as a result of conversations with several close friends to whom I would publicly express my thanks: Christopher Staewen, Käthe and Harald Buchrucker, and my wife.

1

Sexual Love— Human or Divine?

How is the Song of Songs to be read by a Christian, that is, by a member of the community to whom Paul wrote his letters? How are we to reconcile Paul's sayings about love with those ancient love songs traditionally ascribed to the poetic genius of King Solomon?

One answer would be simply not to read the older poems at all. Then there would be no question about how to fit them in with what Paul says. After all, there is no reason for us to try to reconcile all the documents that people have ever written—indeed, that would hardly be possible. Many literary pieces have absolutely nothing to do with each other, and many are even diametrically opposed to one another. There should be no forced harmonization of divergent writings. It is better to leave everything the way it is, openly admitting contradictions where they exist rather than trying to compel agreements in every instance.

But as far as the Song of Solomon is concerned, such an answer is, for the Christian, no solution whatever. After all, this poetic book is unquestionably a part of the Bible—the *graphē,* or Scripture, as Paul respectfully terms it—and since for the Christian everything in the Bible is concerned with Christ and with faith, the Song too can hardly be a matter of indifference.

It is unfortunately true that quarrels broke out from the very beginning between the early Christians and the Jews, and that the early Christians often expressed contempt toward Jews who did not accept Jesus as the Christ. At the same time, however, Christians did something quite amazing. In an act that showed the utmost respect for the Jews, an act that later Christians even to the present day have sometimes regretted and discounted as premature, they accepted as their own the Jewish Bible. Christians actually received their holy book from the Jews! They accepted it as divine revelation, the attestation of God's words and actions. Indeed, they accepted it unconditionally, without any correction, whole and complete, in the very form in which the Jewish authorities themselves had only just finished compiling it, and this Jewish Bible, this Holy Scripture, Christians now called the Old Testament.

And among the writings included in this Jewish-Christian Scripture there is, remarkably enough, a collection of love songs! The Song of Songs is an exchange of endearments between two young people of opposite sex. And in these poems the word *God* occurs only once, and that in a purely formal way ("a flame of Yahweh himself," 8:6 [JB]). Why should that seem surprising? In the love poems you and I recited when we were young the name of God hardly ever occurred either, and no one—not even our heavenly Father—would reproach us for that. But then we make no attempt to include our love poems—or even those of our most famous poets—in the Bible! We keep them in their proper place as *human* writings *outside* the Word of God. They are expressions of *our* hearts, not of the heart of God. Solomon's love songs, however, are different in this respect. They are part of Scripture, and this is why from the outset we cannot avoid the question of how the Christian community should read them—as witnesses to the heart of God *or* as witnesses to the hearts of two young lovers.

And how are we to reconcile what is said about love in 1 Corinthians 13, the New Testament ''Song of Songs,'' with this Old Testament book? Is the word *love* used in both passages in the same sense, for the same sort of love, or is it used for two quite different sorts of love? In our language, as in many other languages, we use one and the same word to designate several quite different realities— God's love for his creatures, Jesus' love for his followers, and the love of a mother for her child, but also at the same time love in the sexual sense, ''sleeping together,'' that is, coitus, or the sexual act.

Either both biblical passages—Paul's ''hymn'' and Solomon's Song—are speaking of the same type of love, *or* the one is speaking of divine love and the other of human love. But if the latter is the case, then what relationship if any is there between the two types of love?

2

Allegorical and Historical Interpretation

For centuries the church, following the example of the Jews from whom Christians had received the Old Testament, opted for the allegorical method of Scripture interpretation. Both Christians and Jews regarded love in the Song of Songs as divine love. The two partners who here declare their love for each other are understood to represent God and humankind, and the love they celebrate can be termed divine. It flows from God to his human creatures and evokes in them a loving response toward their God. Thus, for both Christians and Jews the theme of the Song of Songs was the relationship of mutual love between God and humanity.

Christian interpretation differed from that of Judaism only with regard to the identity of the human partner. For the Jews the love depicted was that between God and Israel, while for Christians it was that between God and his new Israel, the church. For Christians this basic understanding could also vary considerably in form. The God who loved his people could, for example, be God in Christ; thus one could speak of Christ instead of God. And instead of the church one could speak of the Holy Mother as the church's archetype. Or instead of the church as a corporate entity one could speak of the individual Christian, the believing soul, who then becomes the bride exchanging words of love with Christ the bridegroom. Church fathers, medieval theologians, cloistered nuns enraptured by their Christ-mysticism—all gave a great deal of thought to the love poems of the Song of Songs and all found in them—or read into them—their own distinctive piety (and also of course their own repressed sexuality). Protestant piety too made rich and varied use of the texts in the hymn-poems of Tersteegen, Zinzendorf, and Gottfried Arnold, whose melodies of Christian mysticism were often marked by conversations between God and the pious soul.

This particular method of Scripture interpretation is sometimes called "allegory," which means etymologically "another way of reading." The reader must know that in place of the objects, persons, and events specifically *mentioned* in the text other realities are really *meant*. A text that is to be read allegorically is thus a kind of cipher. In order to read it you need a key with which to decipher it. The key is the knowledge of the "real" meaning of the words.

We all use allegorical speech more often than we realize. We use it, for example, in church language when we sing of "Jerusalem the golden," meaning "the home of God's elect," or when we sing, "How brightly beams the morning star," meaning "God's Word feeds us . . . life bestowing." We use allegory also in the language of love, for example, when the Song of Songs speaks of the beloved as a garden, or in all sorts of erotic allusions which we can understand only if we construe the words in a sense different from their surface meaning. The word pictures are allusive, referring to other realities that lie behind them. In the Song of Songs human love poems constitute the foreground, but their real meaning lies behind or beyond them, so that what we hear in the lovers' exchange of words is really a disclosure of the love between the Creator and his creatures, his people.

The allegorical understanding of texts is part and parcel of a world view that prevailed for thousands of years in both East and West until very recent times. Today we find this way of seeing things in terms of "correspondences" quite strange.

According to this ancient view, there is a spiritual world that is higher than the one in which we live. It is the counterpart of the visible world that is accessible to our senses. The spiritual world is the real world, and what we moderns regard as real is only a copy, an illusion of reality. This does not rob the material world of all value. Indeed, by virtue of its correspondence to the spiritual world, the material world becomes a means by which we can know that higher true reality. It is a copy of the original and is the means by which the spiritual world can be represented to us who are confined to the world of our senses. Purely spiritual beings, such as angels, do not need allegory in order to talk with one another about those true, higher realities. But as earthly beings we do need it. We can express what is spiritual only in terms of our senses, and so we can be grateful for the correspondence between the spiritual world and the world of the senses. No one who knows this will place either too high or too low an estimate on this world. To regard it as the sole or principal reality would be to overestimate its value, but to regard it as contemptible or of no value would be just as wrong. The proper estimate sees the world of the senses as a copy through which we can recognize the original and by whose help we inhabitants of this earthly world can express the true reality.

So in order to read the Bible correctly it is necessary to be filled with spiritual knowledge. In his *Confessions* Augustine speaks of the freedom he experienced on learning of the allegorical method of interpreting the Bible. Trained as he was in the philosophy of Plato, Augustine had been offended by the coarsely sensual, all-too-materialistic way in which the Old Testament in particular spoke of God's activity in creation and in history. One example was this Song of Songs, in which two lovers are persuading each other that they should sleep together—what is such a collection of love poems doing in a book of divine revelation? For Augustine's debate partner, who espoused the higher Idealism of ancient philosophy, such biblical passages were proof positive of the inferiority of Judaism and Christianity. Allegorical interpretation helped Augustine and the Christian theologians of his time to overcome these objections and convince contemporary philosophers of the high spirituality of what the Bible says about God. This is why from the time of Origen, who died about A.D. 254, allegory has predominated in the interpretation of the Song of Songs. Allegorical interpretation made it possible for the Song to become a legitimate part of the biblical canon. Modern scholars feel that these ancient love poems were originally written for a quite different purpose, that is, as expressions of purely human, specifically sexual love. But that understanding, if they knew of it, would make no difference to those who use the allegorical method. For them these songs belong in the Bible only because they are capable of being read—allegorically—as dialogues of love between God and Israel, God and the church, Christ and Mary, God and the human soul. Anyone who would construe the poems literally and still regard them as part of the Bible would thereby reveal an ignorance of spiritual matters. He or she would be revealing a carnal mind.

In the Middle Ages, Christian theologians accused the Jews of having carnal minds. To be sure, the Jews, as already noted, also interpreted the Song of Songs allegorically. But there were other biblical passages that Christians alone interpreted allegorically—as referring to Christ, to the Incarnation, and to the future kingdom of God. For example, the figure of David, the royal psalms, the Immanuel passage in Isaiah 7, Jerusalem, Zion, the promised land, and everything that the prophets said about the kingdom of God were all understood allegorically, as prophecies of Christ. The Jews, however, insisted on the literal and historical meaning of these passages and disputed the Christian assertion that their real, basic, higher meaning was with reference to Christ.

At the time of the Reformation, Martin Luther took the revolutionary step of adopting the Jewish approach. He regarded the literal meaning of biblical passages as their true meaning. This had far-reaching consequences. By this revolutionary step Luther removed interpretation of the Bible from its previous Idealistic context and taught us to take our physical world seriously as God's creation: The body is from God. Our bodily existence is not something lower or further removed from God than our spiritual nature, and our spiritual existence is not something higher and closer to God than our bodily nature. Both are part of the nature given us as God's creation. Both are distinguished from God, being as infinitely distant from him as creature is from Creator; yet both are also equally close to God and live in the same way through God's presence. There is no lower and higher; God is just as concerned with the bodily functions of digestion and sex—which Idealism held to be lowly—as he is with our highest thoughts. As

Luther put it, God is present in the intestine of a mouse just as much as in our spirits.

In this way Luther paved the way in Christian theology for the historical-critical method of biblical interpretation. This modern method endeavors to find the literal meaning and thus presents the Song of Songs as a collection of human love songs that from beginning to end speak exclusively of fleshly love.

Do such love poems, then, belong in the Bible, the book that reveals God's dealings with us men and women? It is altogether possible to raise this question without being a prude who thinks love songs are sinful. We all know that in various places the Bible deals quite openly with sexual matters. The question is not whether such a Song belongs in the Bible but whether it isn't superfluous. There are plenty of love songs to be had without going to the Bible. If the Song of Songs is nothing but secular love songs that got into the Bible only because they were mistakenly read allegorically, and if we no longer use allegorical interpretation, then we can simply remove them from the Bible—correct? Or should we assume instead that the Bible *as we have it* is the result of God's concern and provision for his people? If that is our assumption—or hope—then before we remove the Song of Songs from the Bible we should pause and ask if we can perhaps learn something from the fact that the Bible contains these songs. Perhaps we can learn something about earthly love (about sex and eros) as

21

well as about the relationship between earthly love and divine love (eros and agape).

But before we do this, it would not be amiss to say something *positive* about the allegorical interpretation of the Song of Songs if we can, and we can indeed! We are free to do so because allegory is no longer just a way of suppressing sexuality, an expression of how much we are ashamed of sex and of how we would banish it from the realm of fellowship with God. We no longer need deny that what the Song presents is passionate, human love-talk or insist that it was so only originally. On the contrary we can acknowledge that we too are to hear it this way now and take it seriously and joyously. As a result it becomes something glorious for us in that these warmly passionate love songs can be taken as a symbol of the exchange of love between the loving God and humans whom he has awakened to a loving response. Indeed, as allegory the Song casts a light in *both* directions: the flame of sensual love is so beautiful, so free, so acceptable that its intense language can be borrowed to express divine love; and fellowship with God can be so full-blooded, so down-to-earth, so passionate and absorbing, that it finds its appropriate language in the lustiest of human language, the language of the transports of love.

No longer does one method compete with the other. If we base our reflections on what the historical interpretation of the Song of Songs tells us, we do not need to reject or belittle the allegorical, which was basic to Jews and

Christians for centuries. Luther wrote: ''Every Scripture passage is of infinite understanding. Therefore, no matter how much you understand, do not be proud, do not fight against another, do not withstand, because they are testimonies, and perhaps he will see what you do not see. . . . Therefore it is always a matter of making progress in the understanding of Scripture.''

Human-historical interpretation and allegorical interpretation can coexist. Indeed, their coexistence can serve as an indication of the many dimensions of the biblical message. For everything there is more than one referent; there is the horizontal relationship between human beings as well as the vertical relationship between God and humans. So beyond all that we have already observed there is a new dimension of meaning. In a letter from prison Dietrich Bonhoeffer wrote of it in terms of the musical comparison of the melodic theme and counterpoint:

> There is always a danger of intense love destroying what I might call the ''polyphony'' of life. What I mean is that God requires that we should love him eternally with our whole hearts, yet not so as to compromise or diminish our earthly affections, but as a kind of *cantus firmus* to which the other melodies of life provide the counterpoint. Earthly affection is one of these contrapuntal themes, a theme which enjoys an autonomy of its own. Even the Bible can find room for the Song of Songs, and one could hardly have a more passionate and sensual love than is there portrayed (see 7:6). It is a good thing that that book is included in the Bible as a protest against those who believe that Christianity

stands for the restraint of passion (is there any example of such restraint anywhere in the Old Testament?). Where the ground bass is firm and clear, there is nothing to stop the counterpoint from being developed to the utmost of its limits. Both ground bass and counterpoint are "without confusion and yet distinct," in the words of the Chalcedonian formula, like Christ in his divine and human natures.

3

The Affirmation of Sexual Love

In another letter from prison Bonhoeffer wrote: ''I am writing to you in Italy about the Song of Songs. I actually prefer to read it as a worldly love song. That is probably the best 'christological' interpretation.'' Better even than the allegorical interpretation that sees the whole Song as referring to Christ? What could Bonhoeffer have meant by that? I hope that when I have finished, this point will be clearer.

First, a very general statement. It is precisely the Song of Songs that shows us what a great gift God has given us in the historical-critical method of Bible study. If what we have in these poems is a treatment of purely human sexual love, then their presence in the *Bible* demands that the church and all Christians must at long last assume an uninhibited attitude toward sex and eros, that is, we must rejoice that there is such a thing. Sexual desire, one of the most powerful and marvelous of emotions, is a wonderful gift from our Creator.

''Look,'' says the Bible, ''see these two lovers, how they delight in each other, each pleased with the body of the other. How excited they are as each gazes at the full

length of the other's naked body. How they yearn for
night to come so that they can embrace and be united.
They are Adam and Eve in paradise, free of shame, in the
happiness of sex. This is the way it was intended: 'And he
created them man and woman.' How could you possibly
regard that as sinful? Why would you equate sensuality
with immorality? Look at how all their senses are brought
into play—seeing, hearing, smelling, tasting, touching!
This sensuality is the morality of their love because it is
love as God wants it to be, a fully human love, planned for
human beings. There is nothing subhuman or animal
about it, no relic of the earthly to be painfully endured, as
if we had to strive to become purely spiritual beings.
Nothing is so unlike the animals as human sexuality. It is
not confined to times of being in heat, nor does it merely
serve the continuation of the species. It is not limited to
the specific genital activity of procreation but encompasses
the entire person in an act of complete concentration on
and attention to the sex partner. The difference between
man and woman is greater than that between stallion and
mare, and in this difference the man and woman are fully
dependent on and related to each other. Each is bodily
present for the other. Neither is fully human without the
other. The love play of their bodies and their physical
union is both symbol and actualization of their belonging
to each other completely, of their being fully dependent
on and devoted to each other.''

26

Here in this small book of the Bible, then, we have nothing less than the celebration of sensual love. This is the fact of the matter and there is no getting around it.

The two young lovers are not pious. They are not thinking of God, but only of their love—and that in a totally nonreligious way. Had they been singing about their love in a religious manner the songs would have sounded very different. In the nations around Israel at that time the connection between religion and sexuality was of major importance. The gods had offspring as a result of coitus, and the love of god and goddess was the pattern for the love of man and woman. Israel's God, however, is beyond sexuality and is neither man nor woman. The Hebrew language did not even have a word for "goddess." Sex and eros are purely human matters. The nonreligious nature of the Song of Songs is unique in the ancient Near East. "It is a theological achievement of the highest significance that an entire area of life which neighboring religions regarded as a sacral mystery and a divine event is presented here in fully demythologized form." The "theological" achievement of the biblical faith is that it makes the world really world, a nondivine creation. Precisely because of God's goodness as Creator the created world can find joy in life as it is. It is not necessary to elevate life to some religious level, to the level of the divine, before we can affirm it. God's creatures may, indeed should, take pleasure in the life he has given them, even as he does. This understanding, the consequence of God's covenant with Israel, became apparent particularly about the time of Solomon, the period known historically as the "Solomonic Enlightenment" or "Solomonic Humanism." This was a time when Israelites took a new interest in human life and in nature. They looked at the world in a way that is surprisingly modern, nonreligious, secular, in no way to be confused with the divine. The Song of Songs may well not have been written by Solomon, but the poet nonetheless reveals the atmosphere of that age by the way in which he has the two lovers speak of nothing but their love and of that love as being entirely human, physical, sensual.

So let there be an end to any further talk about a "pure" love, purely spiritual, as if that were a higher form of love! The love these two share is not at all "pure" in the sense of being free from sexual desire. On the contrary, they are full of desire; the only thing they want is to go to bed together. "I am weak from passion," they say to each other (2:5; 5:8). We find the man peering through his lover's bedroom window (5:2–6), captivated by what he sees: "The curve of your thighs is like the work of an artist. A bowl is there, that never runs out of spiced wine" (7:1–2). She is delighted with his thighs, which are like alabaster (5:15). Twice she calls out to him, "Come to me, my lover, like a gazelle, like a young stag on the mountains where spices grow'' (2:17; 8:14). Indeed, the Song of Songs concludes on that very note!

Interpreters, in an effort to keep the Song from being construed as immoral, regarded it as the dialogue of a married couple, an extolling of married love. But there is nothing in the text to suggest that the two lovers are husband and wife. On the contrary, it is because they are *not* married that they long for a place where they can sleep together without being disturbed (7:12–8:2).

Toward the end of the last century a German diplomat named Wetzstein appeared to have the solution to this moral dilemma. He reported his observations of oriental marriage customs in Syria and Egypt and how songs there accompany the games and dances during wedding festivities that go on for days at a time. This modern counterpart seemed to suggest that the Song of Songs might be regarded as the text for just such a festival. Individual singers, in alternation with a chorus, were setting forth the love that fills a couple soon to enjoy the pleasures of marriage. But that is just an imaginative way of trying to rescue morality, for in the text itself nothing is said about an impending marriage, and there are no allusions to a wedding. To be sure, the man does address the woman in one context as ''bride'' (4:8–10), but that is only a term of endearment equivalent to ''sweetheart.'' There is no way around it. These two people are simply in love with one

29

another and are planning to sleep together without anyone else's permission, without benefit of marriage license or church ceremony. And *that* is in the Bible!

Interpreters have sometimes clung to one last possibility of rescuing morality and honor, namely, the "biological" explanation that the couple is hoping to have a child, or is at least willing to have one if conception should result. But here in the Song, sex is as far removed from reproduction as it is for many moderns for whom the pill has made "love without worry" a real possibility. There is not a word in the text to suggest that their sleeping together might have any purpose other than the pleasure of the persons involved. There is a world of difference between the Song of Songs and that statement in the Vatican declaration on sexual ethics of 15 January 1976 which says that only through its procreative function does the sex act become "morally good"—that without it, it is something of which we are to be ashamed. A sense of shame, however, is the last thing that would occur to the lovers in the Song of Songs. For them sexual pleasure, quite apart from its biological role in reproduction, is something marvelous, and without the slightest inhibition they proclaim this to the world. Their love is its own legitimation. In the Song of Songs the Bible becomes the ally of all lovers who have no legitimacy other than their love. Their "coming together is not protected by any social sanction; its sole defense is love itself, and after spending

the night together they must expect a painful separation.''
To put it another way: ''In the Song of Songs eroticism
finds itself integrated into the very text of the Bible itself.
. . . Here sexuality becomes lyric, so much so that if the
Song were better known most modern love songs would
seem pale by comparison. The love in question, however,
is completely illicit, and no question whatever is raised
about the mixing of the races: 'Women of Jerusalem, I am
dark but beautiful' (1:5). These two things alone are
reason enough why the Song has been excluded from the
worship orders of the church, especially from marriage services: not only does it present a drama of love that is quite
unconcerned about propriety or moral goodness, but it
also calmly establishes the priority of love over all socially
prescribed rules about bloodlines in marriage (and even
over wedding requirements).''

4

Sexual Desire— God's Good Gift

As far as our attitudes toward sexuality are concerned, the Song of Songs poses for us very sharply the question, How do you feel about illicit sex, the love that has no legitimation except itself? This is the same question that has only recently been posed for the traditional sexual morality of the church by the so-called sexual revolution. Over the past decade or two, members of the younger generation have confronted their elders with a fait accompli in the form of a revolutionary new way of relating freely to one another as male and female. They have rejected as outmoded the norm that had prevailed for thousands of years, by which only lawful sexuality is pleasing to God and anything else is impure and sinful. And the older generation has had to stand by and look on helplessly as sexuality was thus freed from the bonds of legal prescription. Two observations may be made in this connection:

In the first place, the old norm was based on the premise that sexuality is in itself something negative, something that fetters the spirit and holds it down, which

*very hard
and oversimplified*

if not in itself sinful is at best animal in nature. According
to medieval theology—and Luther as well—the transmis-
sion of original sin from generation to generation is tied to
sexual desire. Because its effects were often enough de-
structive of orderly community life (as seen in rivalries and
jealousies that often resulted in killing), much thought
was given to how the sexual drive could be dampened,
channeled, and controlled. To this end it had to be de-
famed and its activity restricted to well-regulated areas of
life. Religion was useful for this purpose, and the Christian
church took an active part in the efforts—all on behalf of
the existing social order which was concerned with the
lawful inheritance of property and privilege. The church
helped in this both by defaming sex and by specifying a
place where sexual activity was permitted, namely, within
that controlled relationship between two persons known as
marriage. Marriage provided both a "remedy for sin" and
an opportunity for having legitimate descendants who
could lawfully inherit property. By rendering this service to
the existing social order the church also ensured its own
dominance inasmuch as the bad name given to such a
powerful natural drive inevitably evoked strong guilt feelings that drove men and women to the confessional.
Through its sacrament of absolution, which alone was able
to allay these guilt feelings, the church thus became indis-
pensable. It had the invincible means of ruling and con-
trolling both soul and mind. This was agreeable to the rul-

ing classes because the church, by reigning in this way, trained the people to accept subservience and affirm the power structure. So far as church and society were concerned, each hand thus washed the other.

Although there is much cause for gloom in today's world, the rediscovery of the Song of Songs could lead us to see that ours is a time filled with new and positive possibilities. For example, the power of the old ecclesiastical sexual morality is broken, and so is the old alliance between church and society. Through the Song of Songs all this is affirmed by the Bible!

In the second place, even though we come to learn how history went awry in some of its developments, and we accordingly give consideration to new and better possibilities, this still does not usher in the kingdom of God. That is to say, today's youth are leaving behind centuries-old problems and restrictions and hypocrisies but, as can be seen today, with new freedoms come new problems. Can the Song of Songs contribute to their solution? Yes, significantly, as we shall see, but not least of all by what it says in the first instance to the older generation.

It speaks to those who share the traditional view of sex with all its buts and reservations and fears and regulations. It tells them, You can say and do something helpful for yourselves and for your youth only if from now on you start with the yes rather than the no and not follow that yes with an immediate *but*—Yes, we agree that sexuality is a part of creation and not something sinful, *but* it is still very dangerous . . . you can't simply say that everything goes . . . you have to structure relationships somehow . . . the sixth commandment must be reaffirmed . . . and on and on.

Behind this "yes, but" lurks that secret quarrel with God which runs through the whole traditional sex ethic: God really could have provided some more reputable and less passionate way of propagating the human race. Had we been the creator, we would have done a better job. But since God arranged it this way, the only thing we can do is at least make sure that nothing worse happens, and to that end we bring sexuality under the umbrella of our norms and codes, and we train our children accordingly. And how does that work out? One result was apparent in the comment of an acquaintance of mine who told her daughter just before her wedding, "If you love a man, you put up even with that!" We are endowed with sexuality, though, not so we will "put up with it" out of respect for the inscrutable but unenjoyable decision of our Creator, but so that we can treasure it as a marvelous gift unique to human life.

"The desire for a woman is God's good gift." Luther said that as a man, speaking only of male desire. The proper wife, of course, was to act as if she had no such desire but was only fulfilling her wifely duty in a spirit of love. In the Song of Songs, however, the woman addresses the man as his equal in every way; she expresses her longing and desire as openly as he does.

According to Karl Barth, what we hear in the Song is ''a voice . . . which we might miss in Genesis 2, that is, the voice of the woman, who looks to the man and goes to him with no less pain and joy than he feels toward her, and who discovers him in freedom equal to that with which he discovers her.''

5

Ordering Sexual Relationship

If the Song of Songs thus extols an illicit kind of love, what can it possibly say to those for whom the distinction between licit and illicit in this connection—and hence also discrimination against the latter—has become a thing of the past? For one thing, if they read the Song carefully they will not find here a carte blanche for the uninhibited living-out of sexuality. They will find some guidelines for life in today's climate of freedom. They have already learned clearly enough that in such a climate it is quite possible for love not only to prosper but also to suffer harm. The old guidelines based on legality and discrimination are gone, and it would not be good to try to reestablish them out of fear or in an attempt to escape the new freedom. These old guidelines, however, did contain an element of truth, that even love requires a structured existence and that sexuality that is not ordered in its expression may seem to prosper but in actuality is only a burden and source of grief. Elements of such a structure, one that is no longer repressive but is consistent with the freedom of the gospel, can be seen in the Song of Songs, precisely because it makes no concessions to rules, is free of them and totally unencumbered.

In the first place, as I have already pointed out, the equality of the woman is striking. In Arabian love poetry we have large numbers of songs in which the male lover describes and admires the beauty of his beloved; it is rare, however, to find the Arabian woman saying anything comparable to what is said by the woman in the Song of Songs (5:10, 16). It is significant and certainly not accidental that the Song actually begins with the passionate words of the woman: "Your lips cover me with kisses; your love is better than wine" (1:2). In the sexual freedom of our day, women are only now for the first time attaining a kind of formal equality under the law. But they are still all too often oppressed, treated as objects, pursued and collected like scalps to enhance some man's reputation, compelled to go along in order to keep up appearances, not allowed to act freely in accord with their own feelings. The Song of Songs clearly points to equality of women.

In the second place, the desires of the two lovers never lead them to pressure one another. The other is always wanted as a person, a partner, not as a thing, a means for sexual gratification. No one is reduced to a mere sex object. All the expressions of affection are appeals to the free emotions of the beloved, voicing the hope that the other will respond with the same love. This concern for the other as person rules out both the brutality of rape and the cunning of seduction, methods designed to bring the other to

40

do something against his or her will, to reduce him or her to a means to an end. Where desire is united with respect for the freedom and equality of the other, hope is a possibility, hope for a free and loving response; what is *not* possible and must necessarily be rejected is compulsion of every sort, no matter how refined.

We have already pointed out that the love portrayed in the Song of Songs is physical, sensual, sexual love. I have stressed this in opposition to a long-standing tendency to spiritualize the Song through capturing it for some mysterious "higher" love and trying to save its morality. Now, however, we must add, in the third place, that this love is also at one and the same time wholly spiritual. To put it more precisely, here is a love that knows no separation of physical and spiritual. The abundance of spirit expressed in the love poems, in their literary artistry, in their metaphors of awe and admiration, demonstrates the spiritual nature of the love itself, its focus on the person of the partner. This partner is not simply a representative of the opposite sex, interchangeable with any other, a mere sex object. The partner is rather a unique and irreplaceable "thou," this *particular* member of the opposite sex, whose place no other could take. Only this man, this woman—this person alone—is loved. The king may have countless queens and "young women without number" at his disposal in his harem, "But I love only one," boasts the man (6:8–9), and he is for her the only one, "the one I love" (1:7; 3:1–3). This physical love is a completely personal love, and this personal love is fully physical and sensual. The older defaming of sex had made a distinction here. On the one hand there was spiritual love directed only to the person, and on the other hand there was the physical satisfaction of sex drives involving use of a partner as means to an end. This is the distinction that is repeated even to the present day in the practice of random promiscuity, which is why promiscuity never results in person-to-person intimacy, never leads to escape from loneliness.

But this very intimacy is precisely the goal of sexual love—the intimacy of two persons in an encounter that is at once both physical and spiritual. This question must at least be kept alive: "Does our being together and our sleeping together lead in that direction?" This question is not intended as a new, repressive commandment or as a condition that must be met before having sex. At stake is rather the hope that the results will be more than merely the pleasure of two bodies. It is this hope that endows the encounter with the possibility of joyful love and makes the partner a unique "thou" who enriches my life and rescues it from self-centeredness. A psychotherapist friend of mine said to me recently when I told him about the public presentation I was to make concerning the Song of Songs, "Tell them to love as much as they can, but not as often as they can."

"My lover is mine, and I am his," the woman sings (2:16; 6:3), and again, "I belong to my lover, and he desires me" (7:10). This complete oneness of sensual and personal love means, in the fourth place, that love's riches are to be found not in oneself but in the other. Each is the source of the other's pleasure. Each has pleasure only by being the source of pleasure for the other. The use of another as a means of attaining one's own pleasure has been done away with altogether. This is not to suggest that desire for the other has been squelched! Desire is still strong, but love has now made it wise. Self-centeredness— I need that person for myself, for my own happiness—is the *power* of eros, whereas the knowledge that I will be happy only through the happiness of my partner is the *wisdom* of eros. Eros understands that we each get what we want, not simply when or if the partner's wants are also met but precisely in and through their being met. In the fullness of this wisdom each of the lovers in the Song of Songs is there wholly for the other, desiring the other completely and yet at the same time totally concerned for the other. Anyone who thinks only of his or her own happiness will miss the riches promised here. But because these riches are to be found in an intimacy involving the whole person, my responsibility for my partner goes beyond the matter of simply assuring that person's pleasure. I am responsible for giving pleasure, but my responsibility does not end there. Finding happiness with another *person* is always more than finding it through *things* such as works of art; it is more because it puts an end to loneliness. It is also riskier and more adventurous because it can never separate the other person from the rest of his or her life, certainly not from

43

the sorrows and burdens that may be forgotten or go unmentioned in the moment of happiness. Sexuality as a relationship between persons brings people together as people, not as things. Being there for the sake of the other thus becomes a condition for one's own happiness. This is what turns sex into eros, into love. And since I take as my partner not some of the other person but the whole person, eros unavoidably enters, as we shall see, into the dimension of agape and becomes subject to agape. Eros and agape are not to be regarded as opposites; they form a unity. This is shown in the Song of Songs, among other things, at the end of the collection, where there is a song which has long been regarded as an expression of Christian agape but which in its present context unquestionably stands as the highest expression of eros:

Set me as a seal upon your heart,
　　as a seal upon your arm;
for love is strong as death,
　　and passion as irresistible as the grave.
Its flashes are flashes of fire,
　　a flame of Yahweh himself,
So that many waters cannot quench love,
　　neither can floods drown it.
Were a man to offer all the wealth of his house to buy love,
　　it would not be enough.

Song of Songs 8:6–7
[translation composite]

44

6
Sex,
Eros, and Agape

Eros, we have suggested, is more than sex. This is true in two respects.

In the first place, sex is a drive governed by our hormones. It demands gratification—"release" as Freud termed it—and to that end any means is satisfactory, whether masturbation, use of an artificial device, sex with an animal, or sex with another person, regardless of whether that person is willing or, as in the case of violent rape, unwilling. We can speak of eros only when more is involved than mere gratification of a hormonal drive, only when the other person is sought as a sensual-spiritual partner. In this sense eros is more than sex.

But that is true in yet a second sense. There are areas of self-development in our lives other than our sexuality. We can speak of eros in other realms of life where our sexuality does not necessarily come into play—unless of course with Freud we assume that sexuality is implicit in all areas of life, in which case, however, it would be "sublimated" and hence only indirectly involved. For instance, there is the love between parents and children or between friends or comrades, there is the teacher's love for a pupil, and the passion of an artist or scholar, a great leader, or a dedicated public servant—all these are forms of human eros. We speak of eros in a wider sense when something we do is marked by strong feelings, warm emotions, and intense personal commitment. We also speak of eros in a narrower sense in the case of day-to-day transactions between two parties—regarding employment, duty, exchange of goods or services—where the relationship is determined not just by an interest in getting the job done but by one's feeling for, attraction to, or concern with the other party as person.

Eros has about it the possibility that ordinary day-to-day relationships can be lifted to a new and higher level of participation and commitment. That is how the human creature has been equipped, with resources for developing and shaping life in a specifically human way. To be sure, eros always makes me concerned also for myself, for the fulfillment of my own needs and desires; to be sure, my erotic longings are always directed also toward what I want, toward what I think will be fulfilling for me. That is to say, eros is concerned with what has value for me and what appears to me to be worth loving, but this by no means automatically makes eros an expression of sin or of selfishness.

If we take seriously the fact that in the Bible eros is allowed to express itself as freely, unreservedly, and openly as it does in the Song of Songs, then we must assume that eros and agape are not to be construed as mutually exclusive. But Protestant theology, from the young Luther, through Calvin, down to Karl Barth, has thought of them that way, strictly on the basis of the command "Love your neighbor as you love yourself" (Matt. 22:39). From the time of Augustine on, this "as you love yourself" was understood in Catholic theology as a recognition that self-love was as justifiable as love of neighbor. The Reformation theologians perceived in such a view a blending of the Greek praise of eros with the biblical call to love one's neighbor. As a result they construed the phrase in a quite different sense: When you lived as the "old man" you were self-centered, but now as the "new man" you can be free of self and find in your neighbor a new center for your life. So for the Reformers it was no longer a case of both/and but a case of either/or—either eros or agape.

But how could this be carried out in practice? After all, the command of self-preservation is also one of God's commands! Self-denial—what Luther called the *odium sui,* or hatred of self—can appeal to Jesus' word that his disciples must hate themselves and father and mother as well if they are to follow Christ (Luke 14:26). This, however, cannot be taken as a comprehensive formula for all of life, because that would lead to paralysis and self-deception, and one bad compromise after another. Jesus' words were directed to critical times of decision, for which his disciples are always counseled, "Let goods and kindred go, this mortal life also.'' In such times the priority belongs to discipleship and making the good confession, to our neighbor and, as Kant would say, duty. But this does not mean that goods, kindred, and life itself are not God's good gifts to be received with joy and gratitude, and hence also objects that we can legitimately desire and strive to possess. Thus the important thing is to give eros, our striving for happiness, its legitimate place in human life, including our life as ''new'' creatures, and this is what Bonhoeffer was trying to do when he wrote from prison that we must learn to think in accordance with the Old Testament first, and only then in accordance with the New.

There are two ways whereby eros can gain its proper place in our lives. First, it can become wise. It can see how its strength is also its peril. Where unenlightened selfishness prevails we trample others and reduce them to means to our ends. A self-centered life reaps the very thing it wants to avoid—loneliness and emptiness. When we grow wise, we recognize that the other person is the partner who can enrich us, and we work for the partner's happiness as the only way whereby we ourselves can be happy. Second, eros is permissible when it is encompassed by agape. Instead of suppressing agape and making itself absolute, eros needs to be ruled and controlled by agape.

But what is agape? How is it different from eros? And how did it come about that there are these two different expressions in Greek which require paraphrase in English, since English—like Hebrew—has only the one word, "love," to cover a wide range of meanings.

The Reformers' sharp contrasting of eros and agape was part of their attempt to do justice to a particularly striking usage they found in the New Testament. In the philosophy of ancient Greece the noun *eros* and the verb *eran* played a large role. These terms designated the human striving for greater and greater accomplishments in the realm of sex as well as in religion, a striving toward those things that promise satisfaction of our longings, fulfillment of our desires, whether for a sexual partner or for the divine. What is striking about the Greek New Testament is that even though much is said in it about love and loving, these two common Greek terms are never used. Indeed, they are deliberately avoided, and in their place the early Christian community adopted a word little used in the other Greek writings of the time, the colorless verb *agapan*, which in meaning somewhat resembles the verb in our expression "I like it." In taking that word and filling it with new meaning of undreamed-of importance, the early Christians were trying to speak of a love about which the Greeks knew nothing. To be sure, people yearned for the gods, but the gods did not yearn for humans, who were so far below them and toward whom they had no desires. Nor does the final ground of all being, whom the Greek philosophers called "God," love people, or any other individual being. He is unmoved and unchangeable. Like a magnet he draws us to himself, but he does not turn to us. He does not love, indeed, he is incapable of love. But the early church was compelled by the revelation of the living God in Jesus Christ to speak of God's love, a love that is actively directed toward us men and women and to all creation. For this love they could not use the words *eros* and *eran,* because this divine love was in no way an erotic love, that is, a love that seeks to enrich its own life through winning that which is lovable. No, God's love seeks nothing for itself. No creature can enrich the creator. God's love is an overflowing love that is "poured out . . . into our hearts" (Rom. 5:5). Much more radically than in the case of eros, this love actually exists for the sake of the other. This is particularly true in the case of God's turning in love to the very creature who has opposed the Creator, that creature in whom erotic striving has become completely self-centered, involving revolt against God and exploitation of other humans, indeed, of all other creatures. Who is this rebellious creature? We are, we human beings. God does not find us lovable. We want to be like God, and when he comes to us we kill him. God has turned in love to precisely this unworthy creature, loving us to the utmost, even to death on the cross. And his love for us is totally unconditional; he loved us while "we were God's enemies" (Rom. 5:10). Such love for enemies can hardly be termed "eros"—it is not a matter of God seeking fulfillment for himself. So the other word, *agape,* came to be used to express the unselfish, self-giving love that God has for those from whom he cannot expect enrichment but only enmity, those whom he does not need in order to live but who urgently need him if they are to regain true life.

Karl Barth wrote, "God could have rested content in himself and in the undisturbed glory and bliss of his inner life. . . . But he did not do this. He chose man to be his partner in a covenant." But what is it that God chose for himself? "When in Jesus Christ he chose man, what did he choose that might bring glory, joy, or triumph? . . . If we want to know what God chose for himself in choosing to be in community with man, our only answer is that he chose our degradation and made it his own. He bore and endured it in every aspect, in its bitterest consequences." What this means is that "God is willing to lose so that man can win. Certain salvation for man, certain peril for God himself! . . . In the choice of Jesus Christ, which is the eternal will of God, God gave man the former, election, happiness, and life, but kept for himself the latter, degradation, condemnation, and death."

In the same sense Luther contrasted human love, that of which the Greek philosophers spoke, with the love of God. Human love is kindled by what we find lovable and it shuns that which we think is bad for us. This is why we seek what is good for us, with the result that we are more concerned with receiving good than with imparting it to

51

others. God's love, however, does not find that which is lovable; it creates it. God loves those who are "sinners, evil persons, fools, and weaklings in order to make them righteous, good, wise, and strong." His love is above all a love that

> flows forth and bestows good. Therefore sinners are attractive because they are loved; they are not loved because they are attractive. . . . This is love of the cross, born of the cross, which turns in the direction where it does not find good which it may enjoy, but where it may confer good upon the bad and needy person. "It is more blessed to give than to receive" [Acts 20:35], says the Apostle.

Thus the nature of agape is clear: agape is unselfish compassion for those who have nothing to offer, at least nothing but harm and enmity, those who seem to be unworthy of love, indeed, worthless altogether. Agape is mercy, tenderheartedness, this last term being Christianity's gift to the language.

By this agape-love, by this pure mercy, we are restored to life. That was the overwhelming experience which gave rise to the writings of the New Testament. It was identical with the discovery that the more we conform to this love, the more we live; the more our eros is permeated by agape, the more our life comes to the fulfillment for which our eros yearns.

In saying this we are not denying the distinction between human love and divine love, of which Luther spoke.

But the relation between them is no longer one of mutual exclusiveness—on the one hand the selfish eros of the "old man" who lays claim to everything and thinks only of his own enrichment, and on the other hand the agape that is not concerned with itself but in compassion works for the well-being of the worthless neighbor and sacrifices itself for him, the love shown by the man or woman who has been made new through God's spirit and imitates the love of God (Eph. 5:1).

If, however, we look at the implications of this marvelous message of God's agape-love for us, we see that we must not automatically equate the divine love with the human. It does not follow that because God's love is not erotic, our human love must become nonerotic, not eros but pure agape. In practice that would be, as I have already said, terribly restrictive, hypocritical, and self-deceptive, because it simply won't work. It is not because we are sinners that it won't work, or because eros is the sinful form of love from which we cannot escape (as the Reformation either/or seems to picture it). No, it won't work because eros is the form love takes in us human creatures, and we cannot escape or even hope to escape from our nature as creatures. A man leaves his father and mother and is united to his wife (Gen. 2:24)—that is eros. It is not a consequence of the Fall; it is rather the beautiful and gracious gift of the Creator, as is the highly erotic love that finds expression in the Song of Songs. Eros as such is not sinful. Eros varies, however, according to whether it is under the dominance of our sinful nature or under the control of the new life that has its origin and sustenance in the love of God.

As sinners we neither know nor care about the love of God, and as a result we are thrown back on our own resources—we ourselves are the sole creators and guarantors of our own happiness. In this anxiety-ridden situation, we live at the expense of the people about us, using them as means for achieving our own happiness. In the eros that is dominated by sin, desire for my own happiness takes priority over the happiness of others.

But what happens when God's agape permeates our eros? We need to be quite clear about this. As long as our striving for happiness is directed toward things—and that can mean anything from good food to treasured works of art—we are still alone, and these things that become the means of satisfying our longings are defenseless against us. But it is a totally different matter when our desires are directed not toward things but toward persons. In the first place, my desires now encounter other desires, and my rights and claims run up against those of another, requests and demands are not only made but also received. Furthermore, only when I am present to serve the desires of the other will that person be present to serve my desires; the path to my happiness leads directly through the happiness of the other person. Human creatures are very much dependent on one another, and the fact that we can find our happiness in the other person only as we are present for that person is nowhere seen more clearly or expressed more intensively than in sexual eros. This is agape, and this is why in interpersonal relationships eros is not replaced by agape, though admittedly every interpersonal encounter raises for us the question of agape—whether and how agape enters into the relationship.

To look at it from the other side, agape, the compassionate, caring, concerned selfless involvement with the neighbor in need of help, cannot be complete if the erotic element is completely excluded. Anyone who has ever shown loving concern for mongoloids, the retarded, the mentally ill can testify how in exercising this compassion and care our human feelings are not excluded; neither can our own desire for sensual satisfaction, for warmth and tenderness, be left out of account. And this is good; it is not something to be ashamed of. Agape does not demand that we repress these feelings, but it does demand that we establish priorities—which is more important, my own satisfaction or the happiness and rights of the other person? This question, which is based on and draws its strength from God's agape-love, takes us beyond our own limits, the boundaries that eros threatens to draw for us. My eros wants the other person to love me, indeed, to live just for me. This is why its strength is sapped when that other person deceives or disappoints me, and even disappears altogether when the other person refuses to love me or perhaps responds to me with hostility, that is, where I can expect from the relationship nothing but pain and grief. Has our love then reached its limit? Is the barrier insurmountable? Yes, according to the Greek philosophers of whom Luther spoke. There is, however, a power that carries our eros beyond this limit, and that is the power of agape, God's spirit of love. ''For when we were still helpless, Christ died for the wicked. . . . We were God's enemies'' (Rom. 5:6, 10). When God turned his love for the neighbor in our direction it became actually love for the enemy. This is why Jesus radically sharpened the Old Testament command to love our neighbor—he made it as comprehensive, unconditional, and unlimited as the love of God himself, which embraces and serves the good and bad alike (Matt. 5:43–48).

God's love for his enemies is the basis for the command that we love our enemies. The word *command*, however, may be subject to misunderstanding. In this connection it does not mean a demand or requirement sure to evoke anxiety. It simply means that if God can do it, so can you! God's action opens up new possibilities for you. If he surmounts barriers, so can you. You are not told of God's unconditional, boundless love just so you can fall down on your knees, marvel at so ideal a love, and be glad that it is extended also to you. On the contrary, the love which for God is reality creates for you a new possibility. This is what is meant by talk about the Holy Spirit, this and nothing less. In this connection just read the fourth chapter of 1 John!

What is possible for God becomes possible for us, but without abolishing the distinction between Creator and creature, between how God relates to us and how we humans with our earthly bodies relate to one another. When the liberating action of the Holy Spirit transforms us, we do not become "like God" (Gen. 3:5)—it was the serpent who promised that. Nor do we become angels, pure spiritual beings. On the contrary, we then become, now at long last, true creatures of the earth, fully part of this world, a condition that Bonhoeffer considered so important. We are free from the "godless fetters of this world," including the fetters of our self-seeking eros, freed for "grateful service to God's creatures." This means also freedom for joyful affirmation of and concern for our own nature as creatures, which includes our sexuality, our desire for sexual happiness, tenderness, intimacy, orgasm, and the physical enjoyment of another person. The love God shows when he forgives us does not negate our nature as physical earthly creatures—that was the error of Neoplatonic Christianity with its defamation of sex. Rather, God's agape affirms our creaturehood. It helps us avoid demonically absolutizing sexuality and eros at the expense of other persons. It frees us to gratefully affirm ourselves and wisely take an interest in the happiness of others, recognizing our own limits and humbly putting our trust in God's love.

Eros and agape are both translated "love," but we need not fault our language for having only one word to serve both meanings. In his novel *The Magic Mountain* Thomas Mann says, "Is it not well done that our language has but one word for all kinds of love, from the holiest to the most lustfully fleshly? All ambiguity is therein resolved: love cannot be but physical, at its furthest stretch of holiness; it cannot be impious, in its utterest fleshliness. It is always itself." Both are types of love, that is, ways of affirming and being present to another person. Eros is the love that is tied to the self; agape is love freed from the self. Eros is thus a conditional love, dependent on what I receive from the other person; agape is unconditional love, called forth not by what the other person can give me but by that person's need for me. In reality, there will not often be a clear distinction between the two. Because agape is not subject to the same conditions as eros, it is freer in reference to persons, places, times, and situations. But it is eros that permeates our life with passion, thrills, tenderness, and excitement and at the same time with danger. Eros is the more endangered and dangerous type of love, and quicksands and pitfalls are always found nearby. Agape, as Paul describes it in 1 Corinthians 13, is never dangerous. It can lead us into great danger, but it is never itself a threat to our life. So it is that we can extol agape as being clearly and undialectically godly and good, whereas eros, because of its dialectical nature, cannot be so praised.

In the kingdom of God the difference between eros and agape will be abolished. It is from this perspective that praise of eros resounds throughout the Bible, beginning already with the marvelous conclusion of the second Creation account: "That is why a man leaves his father and mother [how different from the historically more common practice of having the woman leave home to be married!] and is united with his wife, and they become one" (Gen. 2:24). This practice of eros is heard also in Psalm 45, a royal marriage song that reminds us, however faintly, of the Song of Songs. Then there is that remarkable word of full and free forgiveness bestowed on those caught up in serving the requirements of eros, a forgiveness promised to eros itself, that unprecedented word of Jesus to a woman who had been vilified for illicit eros and who in an erotic manner demonstrated her love for Jesus: "The great love she has shown proves that her many sins have been forgiven" (Luke 7:47). Paul has been misunderstood, and on the basis of some of his statements he has been unjustly criticized as defaming sexuality, but in spite of his advice in a specific situation—"the man who marries does well, but the one who doesn't marry does even better" (1 Cor. 7:38)—as a true Jew he is innocent of the Neoplatonic cult of virginity in the Christian church. For Paul (or, in case Paul is not the author of Ephesians, for a follower of his who understood him well) the eros-love between man and wife is a metaphor of the agape-love between Christ and the church: "A man who loves his wife loves himself. No one ever hates his own body. Instead, he feeds it and takes care of it, just as Christ does the church" (Eph. 5:28–29). And then he reminds his readers of Gen. 2:24 by quoting the passage directly (5:31). So we see that the words of eros, where it has reached its fullest and best development, are identical with the words of agape. In writing 1 Corinthians 13, Paul may have had in mind that which eros can both say and promise, "Set me as a seal upon your heart . . . love is strong as death" (Song of Songs 8:6, RSV).

7

Sex and Society

Society's interest in an ordered sexual relationship is also illumined by the two lovers of the Song of Songs, though not by anything we see and hear of them directly. What we see and hear is their moment of happiness, their mutual enjoyment. We stand nearby and hear with delight their expressions of endearment. "Seeing two lovers is like watching a drama fit for the gods," wrote Goethe in *Stella*. That's right. It's a scene to make the heart rejoice, and even the Bible offers us this joy.

But life is more than such a moment of joy, and each of these lovers expects from the other more than just a moment of shared happiness. Both regard their love as something eternal. The eternity of which it partakes is that of the full and blessed moment—beyond which, while we are actually experiencing it, we cannot see or think of anything else. Nietzsche said, "Desire always intends eternity": strong love always desires to continue indefinitely and to encompass the entire person now and in the future. The person whom I erotically desire is a total being, however, who brings to me not just the beauty and love extolled in the Song of Songs but also everything that lies hidden behind, beneath, and beyond that beauty and love—ugliness and the limits of love, selfishness and sorrow, cares and fears, in short, all the burdens of life and, implicit in them, the burdens that only the future will disclose. Observing two such lovers we might wish:

> O, were it ever green! O, stay,
> Linger, young Love, Life's blooming May!

But the two persons do not remain young, and the question we must put to eros is, Will their love be "ever green"? That's where agape comes in; that's the question agape puts to eros.

All these concerns are blocked out in the joy of that full and blessed moment, but they are nonetheless there. And it is a good thing that they are. Otherwise eros, which here sings so happily, could run into trouble of two kinds.

First, eros might desire from the partner only what is beautiful, only what gives delight. In the Song of Songs the man says, "How pretty you are, how beautiful; how complete the delights of your love" (7:6). "How beautiful you are, my love; how perfect you are!" (4:7; see also 1:15; 4:1; 6:4). In like manner she speaks to him, "How handsome you are, my dearest; how you delight me!" (1:16), and says of him, "His mouth is sweet to kiss; everything about him enchants me. This is what my lover is like, women of Jerusalem" (5:16). A person who feels only erotic love is unprepared to put up with the burdens of the beloved and so can accept the other only halfway, only when the beloved gives pleasure. But that is to accept an object that enriches rather than a living person or partner—something that no partner, no person, deep down could ever want. When we enter a relationship our hope and unexpressed wish is always to be fully accepted, even to the point of being helped in the carrying of our burdens. Thus in the erotic encounter the question of agape is always present from the outset.

Second, it is said that lovers are all alone in the world. They are so taken up with each other that they forget everything else. The world about them, if it exists at all, exists only as a foil for bringing out the superior qualities of the beloved. For the man, his beloved is unique, the most beautiful of women (5:9; 6:8–9). For her he is "like an apple tree among the trees of the forest" (2:3), "one in ten thousand" (5:10). The other persons in the poems are merely decorative embellishments—the mother, the brothers, the women, the king with his harem, even the city watchmen (3:3; 5:7).

None of this, however, can alter the fact that the lovers, as surely as they are caught in the flow of time, are also members of society. They are timeless in the sense that they speak for the lovers of every age; yet they are also unmistakably children of their own time and their own social stratum, the court and the upper class of Solomon's empire. Caught up in mutual admiration, they can regard themselves as an elite couple, far removed from all the lesser mortals around them. They are sufficient unto themselves as they sit on the hill of happiness above the rest of humanity and bask in the envy of those less fortunate, whom they regard as unhappy intruders on their love.

In either case eros is in trouble. It loses the opportunity of existence for the sake of another and therewith the possibility of being enriched by others. It is thrust into the loneliness of self-centeredness. Eros must always face the question put by agape: Are we prepared to accept the hurts and pains as well as the hopes and pleasures that we bring to one another, and do we mean to keep our happiness to ourselves alone, letting it cut us off from others, or will we instead allow it to open us up to others, especially those less fortunate and less happy than ourselves?

It will not be long until the lovers are no longer alone and society invades their love. They will be responsible to society for their love, and they will be forced to bring their love into conformity with society's rules—or assert it in defiance of those rules. They will see that sleeping together is more than just a pleasure in which they can forget everything else—that it has real consequences: children. And if not sooner, then at least later when children come, the couple will see that their love concerns persons other than themselves, namely, the children and everyone who has reason to be interested in them individually or as a couple—their families, their society, their nation. Their love thus goes beyond itself in time and space. Their moment of love is extended beyond the particular moment and place toward the future and outward into the world around them, and as a consequence it requires a structuring other than that dictated by the spirit of love alone. Thus their life together brings them face-to-face with the question of institutionalization. Because human life is lived in time and in society it can be lived only in and through institutions, which involve structures and regulations that can ensure continuity and duration as well as a clear and continuing interconnection with the larger human community.

That here in the Song there is no thought at all of children reminds us, as I said earlier, that the legitimacy and moral goodness of sexual eros and its physical fulfillment does not depend in the first instance on procreation, as the Vatican declaration states. On the contrary, it is meaningful and right because its intense intimacy expresses in a most powerful way our created nature as sexual beings, quite apart from any purpose to propagate the species. But the possibility that children may result from our sleeping together reminds us from the outset that while our happiness in love may seem to be a purely private matter, it really is not. In reality, this most intimate, private, and personal relationship is at the same time an event of significance for society—because of the children that may be born; because our lives are inevitably intertwined with those of others who have claims on us, even on the two of us as we are together in love; and finally because a drive as powerful as the sexual drive always has consequences for the life of the whole human community. This is why society cannot ignore sex and the sexual relationship, as if it were the private concern of the lovers, but must adopt a position toward it. Society asks the lovers if they are now ready and willing to regard themselves as permanently paired and to confirm their life together by assuming special rights and duties. And society shows its interest in their faithfulness. It wants them to assume responsibility for each other and not immediately to go their separate ways again as soon as they run into difficulty. It asks that they determine to stay together ''for better and for worse,'' yes even ''until death do us part.''

The question of agape has led us to the question of the institutionalization of sexual eros and how love in its freedom relates to the institution of marriage. At this point the present discussion must end because at this point—today more than ever—a host of questions arise to which we can just now hardly begin to suggest an answer. At least two things, however, need to be said anyway, two things that are important for any correct *approach* to these questions. They need at least to be mentioned here particularly because of the way people have tried for thousands of years to institutionalize love by way of the ordinances of marriage, seeking to bring the sexual drive, and along with it sexual eros, under the control of society and whatever its overriding interest may happen to be at any given time.

Although the question of the institutionalization of marriage cannot and should not be avoided—indeed, as we have seen, it is explicitly posed by the involvement of agape in the eros relationship—it is crucial that we not deny or diminish the propriety in its own right of that great event, the sexual encounter of two human beings. Neither may we place it under legal restraints, as if love acquired its right, including its right to physical consummation, only through some kind of authorization and otherwise had no right to happiness and consummation. That is the way it has usually been, even in the church's understanding of sexual morality. Concerning all the tragedies that have occurred as a result we can say with Goethe, ''The many offered here / are neither lamb nor steer / but human sacrifice beyond belief.'' In the unsanctioned love of the Song of Songs, the Bible tells us that all our attempts to structure and regulate sexual eros must be considered as helps, not conditions. Love is not legitimized by legal sanction. It needs no marriage license or church ceremony. Laws concerning it should aim only at helping it fulfill its own wish to be something that is not merely private but public and significant for the society in which we live. This is the first thing to be said: love legitimates itself.

There is a second matter of equal importance. Nothing, it would appear, is quite so resistant to categorization in general terms and measurement against general norms as the life of sexual eros. But traditional sexual morality routinely works with just such general categories and norms. They make everything so convenient; we can judge and decide even without close examination because anything not legally sanctioned is obviously illegitimate. That is the language of law, which forces each individual case into the procrustean bed of the general norm, even if that can be accomplished only by doing violence to the persons involved. The law brings only wrath (Rom. 4:15) and hypocrisy, all kinds of secret transgressions, and the whole hodgepodge of the double standard.

In those areas where general norms are both possible and necessary, for example, in the realm of economics and social policy, the church has unfortunately declared itself incompetent to speak; it has recognized the autonomy of those realms and restricted itself to empty generalizations. In the realm of sexual eros, on the other hand, it has recognized no such autonomy but has zealously set up very strict and detailed norms, enforcing them with highly repressive methods. According to these norms, even the two lovers of the Song of Songs fall short, because the norms tie everything to some formal authorization and urge every lover, "For the consummation of love you must await appropriate sanction, and if such sanction should for some reason not be possible, then you must forego consummation altogether." What we should learn from the Song of Songs is that precisely in this area the individual case is not under the general law but above it. Each pair of lovers is a unique case. As the Spirit moves where he will, so does love move where it will. This comparison is neither accidental nor blasphemous. The same church that wants to make love dependent on legal sanction has also been concerned wherever possible to bring the Spirit of God under its dominance and make the Spirit move through the church's channels. It has had the same mistrust of the free movement of the Spirit and what the Spirit might accomplish as it has had of the freedom of eros, that unpredictable vagabond. In reference to both areas the church, indeed, all of us, must learn that the most important thing is to be attentive to ways in which we can *help* each other. And in cases of love, we must take each case on its own terms, remind every couple of the agape question which is implicit in their togetherness, and let authorization serve as an aid to a life in which love will be enduring, whole, and of benefit to the larger world of which it is a part.

8

The Song of Songs— A Magna Charta of Humanity

Because the fear of freedom is so deeply rooted in us, it takes courage to follow this path. Is that fear likely to be diminished by our opening up a broader vision? I really don't know. I hesitate even to mention this larger vision because there is so little hope of realizing it. But then there is always the Song of Songs! So mention it I must. The vision is that which Kurt Marti, the poet-pastor from Berne, Switzerland, has called an "erotic culture of peace." Mentioning it may at least help keep this brief interpretation and application of the Song of Songs from being quietly buried, or even twisted beyond recognition in the bickering of those who see it, whether approvingly or disapprovingly, as a carte blanche for sexual license. More important, there is a real question whether our understanding of sexuality has any relevance for the deep cultural crisis of our time and for the much-debated quest for a new life-style, and whether traditional sexual morality offers an adequate basis for our approach to that crisis and that quest.

Related to this matter of sexuality are all sorts of other

developments in our fast-moving society with its shifting interests. I would mention here but two of them, two that are closely interconnected, namely, the exclusion of women from the male world and the exclusion of feelings from public as over against private life. In these respects, the Christian denominations have little ground for pointing the finger at one another. No one church has done better than another; all have operated under the prejudice of a Neoplatonic hostility to the body and to sex. Each may have expressed the prejudice differently, but all alike gave legitimacy to male dominance and fostered the twin exclusions instead of opposing them, as would have been demanded by the wonderful mutuality which characterized the relationships between men and women in the early Christian community.

"Who directs or who permits [males and females] to run from each other?" asks Karl Barth. "That this won't work is demonstrated in the fact that every artificially introduced or maintained separation of the sexes tends to make the men barbaric, the women affected, and both somewhat inhuman." We need only examine the numerous portraits of famous generals, business tycoons, and celibate clerics, that is, men who in their daily work had no close female colleagues, to discover as the young Friedrich Schleiermacher put it in his defense of Friedrich Schlegel's novel *Lucinde*: "Wherever women are out of the picture everything inevitably becomes coarse."

Through the rational elements in its doctrine of vocation, Protestantism, as Max Weber has suggested, was closely linked with bourgeois society and the rationality of capitalistic production, so much so as to nullify the effects of Luther's openness to "God's good gift" of sexuality, or at least limit it to a respect for marriage and for the proper housewife. Our present equality of women under the law came about despite the church's resistance. And it has not achieved a great deal beyond the inclusion of the woman, for purposes of economic productivity, in the man's world—where she must now "work like a man."

The commercial world in which we live transforms all human relationships into cold and impersonal business transactions. Given a permissive society such as we have today with its sexual license, sex too is immediately drawn into the business category of sexual performance and into the commercialism of the giant pornography enterprise. It is useless to invoke traditional sexual morality against this "decay of morals," or to agitate for higher standards and stricter divorce laws. Because we regard the capitalist system of production as inviolable, we are blind to how it has bred and nurtured these developments. Indeed, traditional morality itself has contributed to that increase of coarseness and barbarism in human relationships about which Barth and Schleiermacher spoke. It did this by excluding women from areas of life that men had reserved for themselves and by showing contempt for feelings, espe-

73

cially erotic feelings, expressed outside the legalized privacy of marriage.

Thus the present liberation of sexuality from its old chains is a mixed bag. It has resulted both in the perversion of sex into a commercial transaction and in the dawn of that "erotic culture" envisioned by Marti, a culture in which there is a reduced emphasis on productivity and performance—which have already been carried to the point of self-destructive absurdity—and greater emphasis on "the development of freer, less goal-oriented, indeed, even purposeless creative capabilities and activities," obviously with "the destruction of the existing value system" as a presupposition: "Any culture and especially an erotic culture, if it is to endure, must begin by eliminating all exploitation. If participation is not open to all and only an elite achieves fulfillment, the happiness of an erotic society will be ephemeral, and any hopes connected with it are bound to be dashed."

Heinrich Böll once expressed a desire for what he called a theology of tenderness:

Implicit in the New Testament is a theology of, I dare to say, tenderness. This tenderness invariably effects healing, whether by word, by the laying on of hands—which could also be called "stroking"—by kisses, or by a shared meal. In my opinion, all this has been stifled and lost to us by a perverse process of legalization, we could almost say, by

74

What of Frances of Assisi etc. ?

Romanism, which turned it into dogmas and principles and catechisms. This New Testament element of tenderness has yet to be rediscovered. All we have instead is people snarling and snapping at each other, bawling each other out.

On another occasion Böll called it a theology of the tenderness of Mary Magdalene, the woman to whom much was forgiven because she loved much. And once he wrote:

> The saying "You have sorrow now, but you will rejoice" must be related to the sexuality of *both* sexes. . . . I cannot imagine how many joyless marriages, how many joyless performances of marital duty there may have been, whole continents full of formless or unformed contents. . . . It doesn't take great psychological or psychiatric experience, merely a little imagination, to have some idea of the number of people in whom the joylessness of their sexuality has gone as far as illness—and how many have been cured by pleasure in it.

This then is the expansive vision that the Song of Songs opens up: on the horizon ahead, the longed-for utopia of a liberated and human culture in which the gifts we have as God's creatures, though stifled now, can flourish; and on the inner horizon, personal relationships that prosper erotically because of the mutual permeation of eros and agape. The fact that we have not yet learned this shows clearly why it is both right and necessary for the Song of Songs to be in the Bible. Karl Barth was correct in calling it, along with the second account of Creation in Genesis 2, a second "Magna Charta of humanity." "We should not wish to take it out of the canon. Neither should we act as if it were not in the canon, or spiritualize it as if everything in the canon could have only spiritual significance. . . . Here the most natural interpretation might well prove to be the most profound."

Notes

Page

23 LUTHER: Martin Luther, "First Lectures on the Psalms:
    Psalms 76–126," ed. Hilton C. Oswald, trans. Herbert
    J. A. Bouman in *Luther's Works,* ed. Jaroslav Pelikan and
    Helmut T. Lehmann, 55 vols. (Philadelphia: Fortress Press;
    St. Louis: Concordia, 1955–), 11:433.

24 BONHOEFFER: Dietrich Bonhoeffer, *Prisoner for God: Letters
    and Papers from Prison,* ed. Eberhard Bethge, trans. Regin-
    ald H. Fuller (New York: Macmillan Company, 1960),
    p. 131, in a "letter to a friend" dated 20 May 1944.

25 BONHOEFFER: Dietrich Bonhoeffer, *Widerstand und Erge-
    bung: Briefe und Aufzeichnungen aus der Haft,* ed. Eber-
    hard Bethge, new ed. (Munich: Chr. Kaiser Verlag, 1970),
    p. 345, in a letter dated 2 June 1944.

27 "IT IS A THEOLOGICAL ACHIEVEMENT . . .": Gillis Gerleman,
    Das Hohelied, Biblischer Kommentar, Altes Testament
    (Neukirchen-Vlyun: Neukirchener Verlag des Erziehungs-
    vereins, 1973), 18: 84.

30 VATICAN DECLARATION: "A Declaration on Some Questions
    of Sexual Ethics," issued by the Sacred Congregation for
    the Doctrine of the Faith on 29 December 1975 and first
    released in Rome on 15 January 1976. See the text in *The
    Pope Speaks* 21, no. 1 (1976), especially pp. 63–64.

31 "Coming together . . .": Gerleman, *Das Hohelied,* p. 120, in commenting on the Song of Songs 2:6.

31 "In the Song of Songs . . .": George Crespy, "Pour une théologie de la sexualité," in *Études théologiques et religieuses* 52, no. 1 (1977): 110.

37 Barth: Cf. Karl Barth, *Church Dogmatics,* ed. G. W. Bromiley and T. F. Torrance, 4 vols. in 11 (Edinburgh: T. & T. Clark, 1936–69), 3^2: 294.

47 Barth: See ibid., 4^2: 733–36.

48 Bonhoeffer: *Prisoner for God.* See esp. the letters dated Advent II, 1943 (p. 79); 30 April 1944 (p. 124); 20 May 1944 (p. 131); 27 June 1944 (pp. 153–54); 28 July 1944 (p. 173).

51 Barth: Cf. *Church Dogmatics,* 2^2: 166, 164, 162–63.

52 "Sinners, evil persons, . . .": Martin Luther, "Heidelberg Disputation, 1518," trans. Harold J. Grimm, *Luther's Works,* 31: 57.

52 "Flows forth . . .": Ibid.

57 "Godless fetters . . ." "Grateful service . . .": *Theological Declaration concerning the Present Situation of the German Evangelical Church,* adopted by the Synod of Barmen, 29–31 May 1934, sec. 2. See the text in Arthur C. Cochrane, *The Church's Confession under Hitler* (Philadelphia: Westminster Press, 1962), p. 240.

58 Mann: Thomas Mann, *The Magic Mountain,* trans. H. T. Lowe-Porter (New York: Alfred A. Knopf, 1953), p. 599.

62 "O, were it . . .": Johann Christoph Friedrich Schiller, "The Lay of the Bell." See the text in Thomas Carlyle, *Schiller,* trans. Edward Lytton Bulwer (Boston: Houghton, Mifflin and Company, 1881), p. 20.

72 Barth: Cf. *Church Dogmatics,* 3^4: 165–66.

74 "THE DEVELOPMENT . . . TO BE DASHED": Kurt Marti, "Das erotische Verhältnis des Schriftstellers zur Sprache," in *Grenzverkehr. Ein Christ im Umgang mit Kultur, Literatur, und Kunst* (Neukirchen: Neukirchener Verlag, 1976), pp. 46, 49.

75 BÖLL, "IMPLICIT IN . . .": Heinrich Böll and Christian Linder, *Drei Tage im März, Ein Gespräch* (Cologne: Kiepenheuer und Witsch, 1975), p. 72.

75 BÖLL, "THE SAYING . . .": Heinrich Böll, "About Joy," in Johann Baptist Metz and Jean-Pierre Jossua, eds., *Theology of Joy*, Concilium 95 (New York: Herder and Herder, 1974), pp. 154–55; trans. Francis McDonagh; italics by Böll.

76 BARTH: Cf. *Church Dogmatics*, 3^2: 293–94.